THE COOK'S COLLECTION
❋

DELICIOUS
FISH

Author: Annette Wolter
Photography: Susi and Pete Eising
   (photo page 42 by Odette Teubner)
Translated by UPS Translations, London
Edited by Josephine Bacon

CLB 4159
This edition published in 1995 by Grange Books
an imprint of Grange Books PLC, The Grange, Grange Yard, London SE1 3AG
This material published originally under the series title "Kochen Wie Noch Nie"
by Gräfe und Unzer Verlag GmbH, München
© 1995 Gräfe und Unzer Verlag GmbH, München
English translation copyright: © 1995 by CLB Publishing, Godalming, Surrey
Typeset by Image Setting, Brighton, E. Sussex
Printed and bound in Singapore
All rights reserved
ISBN 1-85627-740-2

THE COOK'S COLLECTION

✳

DELICIOUS FISH

Annette Wolter

Grange
BOOKS

Introduction

Fish has always been popular, but it is only recently
that its various qualities have been fully
appreciated. Not only is fish healthy, and quick and
easy to cook, it is also available in a surprising variety
of shapes, sizes and flavours. In recognition of this,
most large supermarkets now have fish counters,
generally with a good selection of home and foreign
produce with which to experiment.

Fresh fish can be expensive, but since there is so
little waste when cooked, it can still work out to be
an economical choice. A really fresh fish is slimy and
slithery with a bright eye and black pupil, firm,
elastic flesh and clean red gills, whereas a stale fish
looks dull, has sunken eyes with grey pupils and
dirty, dark gills. Shellfish too should look clean and
bright. Cooked shrimps and crabs should be bright
red. Lobsters and crabs should be good and heavy,
and the tail and claws should still be springy,
indicating that they were alive before being boiled.
Shellfish, such as mussels and oysters, should be
firmly closed if bought alive. Any open shells must
be discarded. All fresh fish and seafood should be
cooked and eaten on the day of purchase.

Versatility is one of the great attributes of fish. It is
not simply the fact that there are countless methods
of cooking fish, but it is also a wonderful primary
ingredient for any occasion. It is always fun to marry
fish to new flavours and to experiment with herbs,
spices and sauces. This exciting collection of fish
recipes will inspire keen fish cooks and novices alike
to widen their culinary repertoire with delicious and
uncomplicated fish and seafood dishes.

Each recipe serves four, unless otherwise indicated

Chinese Fish Soup

100g/4oz carrots
500g/1lb 2oz Chinese cabbage
2 tbsps sesame oil
100g/4oz brown rice
4 tbsps soy sauce
100g/4oz shelled green peas
200g/7oz canned soya bean
sprouts
500g/1lb 2oz cod fillet
2 tbsps lemon juice
3 pinches of five-spice powder
2 tbsps finely chopped fresh dill

Preparation time:
1 hour
Nutritional value:
Analysis per serving, approx:
• 1190kJ/285kcal
• 28g protein
• 6g fat
• 27g carbohydrate

Wash and clean the carrots and Chinese cabbage, then cut them into strips. • Heat the oil in a large pan. Fry the rice for 5 minutes. Add the prepared vegetables and fry for a further 5 minutes. Add 1 l/1³/₄ pints of hot water and 2 tbsps of soy sauce and simmer for 20 minutes. • Add the peas and soya bean sprouts. • Wash the fish and squeeze the lemon juice over it, then cook it on the bed of vegetables for 10 minutes or until tender.
•Remove the fish and break it into pieces with a fork. Remove the pan from the stove. Season the soup with the remaining soy sauce and five-spice powder. Stir in the dill and fish chunks.

Our Tip: Soy sauce is an indispensable ingredient in oriental cookery. Shoyo and Tamari are brands available in health food shops which are both naturally produced and therefore especially aromatic.

Fish Soup with Croûtons

750g/1lb 10oz freshwater fish
such as carp, pike or eel
1¹/₂l/2¹/₄ pints water
1 tsp salt
4 tbsps vinegar
2 onions
1 bay leaf
8 peppercorns
100g/4oz carrots
100g/4oz parsley
3 tbsps flour
2 tbsps oil
1 tsp paprika
100ml/4fl oz sour cream
Salt and white pepper
1 tbsp chopped fresh parsley
2 slices white crustless bread
15g/¹/₂ oz butter

Preparation time:
30 minutes
Cooking time:
45 minutes
Nutritional value:
Analysis per serving, approx:
• 1715kJ/410kcal
• 38g protein
• 20g fat
• 18g carbohydrate

Clean the fish and wash thoroughly under running water. Chop it coarsely and cook in salted water over a low heat for about 20 minutes or until tender, together with the vinegar, onions, bay leaf and peppercorns. • Scrape, wash and slice the carrots and coarsely chop the parsley. Strain the fish liquid, add the vegetables and allow it to cook for 15 minutes. • Heat the oil and stir in the flour. Fry until golden, add the paprika and pour in the liquid, stirring constantly. Bring the soup to the boil briefly, stir in the sour cream and season it with salt and pepper. Separate the fish flesh from the bone and heat the pieces in the soup. Stir in the parsley. • Cut the bread into cubes and fry in butter until golden. Serve the soup sprinkled with croûtons.

Dutch Eel Soup

To serve 6:
750g/1lb 10oz fresh eel
750ml water
½ tsp salt
500ml/16fl oz dry white wine
1 untreated lemon, washed
1 tbsp flour
25g/1oz butter
2 tbsps capers
1 tbsp chopped fresh parsley
Salt and freshly ground white pepper
Pinch of sugar
1 tbsp lemon juice
2 egg yolks
120ml/4fl oz cream

Preparation time:
10 minutes
Cooking time:
25 minutes
Nutritional value:
Analysis per serving, approx:
• 2110kJ/505kcal
• 20g protein
• 43g fat
• 3g carbohydrate

Wash the eel thoroughly and cut it into chunks. • Add the eel to the salted water and bring it to the boil. Cook for 15 minutes in an uncovered pan, skimming regularly. • Add the wine and one half of the lemon to the eel and simmer for 5 minutes. Remove the pieces of eel from the liquid, separate the flesh from the bones and keep warm. Strain the liquid. • Fry the flour in the butter, stirring constantly. Gradually add the liquid and bring to the boil. Stir the capers and parsley into the soup and season with salt, pepper, sugar and lemon juice. • Beat the egg yolks with the cream, add a little of the soup, then thicken the soup with this mixture. Add the pieces of eel to the soup. Thinly slice the rest of the lemon and add a few bits to the liquid. Garnish with some julienne strips of lemon rind if desired. Serve piping hot.

Cream of Scampi Soup with Chives

4 small tomatoes
4 shallots
2 tbsps butter
1 tbsp flour
6 tbsps dry white wine
250ml/8fl oz hot chicken stock
400ml/15fl oz single cream
Pinch each of salt and sugar
Pinch of freshly ground white pepper
5 drops Tabasco sauce
250g/8oz freshly peeled scampi
2 bunches chives

Preparation time:
40 minutes
Nutritional value:
Analysis per serving, approx:
• 2130kJ/510kcal
• 15g protein
• 42g fat
• 15g carbohydrate

Wash the tomatoes, cut a cross in each top and bottom, then plunge them briefly into boiling water. Skin them, cut them in half and remove the pips. Cut the flesh into small cubes. Chop the shallots very finely and fry in the butter until transparent. Add the flour and fry, stirring constantly, dilute with the white wine. Stir in the chicken stock and add the cream. Allow the soup to come to the boil briefly, then season it with the salt, sugar, pepper and Tabasco sauce. Leave over a gentle heat for 5 minutes. • Heat the washed prawns and diced tomatoes in the soup. Wash the chives, pat them dry and chop finely; stir about 2 tbsps of chive rings into the soup. • Serve the soup in heated soup plates, sprinkled with the remaining chives.

Cucumber and Dill Soup with Shrimp

1 onion
1 clove of garlic
30g/1oz butter
1tsp flour
375ml/14fl oz meat stock
1 cucumber
375ml/14fl oz cream
Pinch each of salt, sugar and white pepper
Pinch of mustard powder
200g/7oz shrimps in their shells
2 bunches of dill

Preparation time:
30 minutes
Nutritional value:
Analysis per serving, approx:
• 960kJ/230kcal
• 11g protein
• 17g fat
• 7g carbohydrate

Chop the onion and garlic finely and fry in 10g/¼oz of butter until transparent. Add the flour, fry until bright yellow, then add the stock. Wash the cucumber, trim the top and tail and cut off four think slices. Reserve them. Peel the remaining cucumber, cut it in half along its length, scrape the seeds out with a spoon and chop the flesh into 2cm/¾-inch cubes. Boil the cucumber cubes in the liquid for 15 minutes. • Purée the soup in a liquidiser. Add the cream. Season well with salt, sugar, pepper and mustard powder and simmer over a gentle heat for 5 minutes. • Peel and de-vein the shrimps. • Heat the remaining butter in a pan and fry the shrimps briefly. Wash and chop the dill, then stir it into the soup. • Pour the soup into heated soup plates and add the shrimps and cucumber slices.

Solyanka

1 onion
375g/12oz floury potatoes
1 bunch pot herbs (leek, carrot, turnip, swede, etc.)
2 tbsps olive oil
4 tbsps wholewheat flour
1 tsp mushroom ketchup
2 tbsps tomato purée
1 bay leaf
1 l/1³/₄ pints hot water or meat stock
500g/1lb 2oz redfish or cod fillet
250g/8oz pickled gherkins
250g/8oz beef tomatoes
4 tsps capers
200ml/6fl oz sour cream
1-2 tbsps soy sauce
1-2 tbsps mushroom ketchup
1 tbsp lemon juice
2 tbsps finely chopped fresh dill

Preparation time:
20 minutes
Nutritional value:
Analysis per serving, approx:
• 1525kJ/365kcal
• 29g protein
• 14g fat
• 29g carbohydrate

Dice the onions and potatoes. Wash, clean and chop the pot herbs. • Heat the oil in a large pan. Fry the prepared vegetables. Sprinkle with flour and mushroom ketchup, add the tomato purée and bay leaf and stir. Gradually add the water or stock, bring to the boil and stir until smooth. • Wash the fish and add to the soup. Cook for 10 minutes over gentle heat until tender. • Dice the gherkins and cut the washed tomatoes into eighths • Break the fish into chunks and divide it between four heated plates. Add the capers, gherkins and tomatoes to the soup and allow them to cook for about a minute. Remove the pan from the heat. Beat the sour cream with the soy sauce and lemon juice and stir into the soup. • Serve the Solyanka with a sprinkling of fresh dill.

Norwegian Fish Mould

750g/1lb 10oz cod or redfish
1 day-old bread roll
250ml/4fl oz milk
40g/1¹/₄oz streaky bacon
1 onion
3 eggs
1 tbsp cornflour
Pinch each salt and freshly
grated nutmeg

Preparation time:
30 minutes
Cooking time:
1 hour
Nutritional value:
Analysis per serving, approx:
• 1965kJ/470kcal
• 45g protein
• 25g fat
• 16g carbohydrate

Wash and dry the fish, then cut it into coarse cubes. Soften the bread roll in 125ml/4 fl oz milk. Dice the bacon and finely chop the onion. • Fry half the bacon in its own fat in a pan. Sweat the onion in the bacon fat until it turns yellow, then set aside to cool. • Put the fish cubes, diced bacon, fried bacon and onion mixture through a mincer. Mix to a stiff paste with the eggs, the remaining milk, the cornflour and the bread roll, lightly squeezed out; season with salt and nutmeg. • Grease a jelly mould and sprinkle with breadcrumbs. Fill with the fish mixture and cover tightly. Place the mould in a water bath over a gentle heat for 1 hour. Take care that the water reaches no higher than about 3cm/1 inch below the edge of the pudding mould. • Remove the mould from the water. Leave to stand for a few minutes, then turn out and serve immediately. • Tastes excellent with a spicy tomato or herb sauce.

Gravad Lax

To serve 8:
1kg/2¼lbs fresh salmon (centre cut if possible)
1½ tbsps caster sugar
2 tbsps coarse salt
1 tsp freshly ground white pepper
3 bunches dill
1 lemon

Preparation time:
20 minutes
Marinating time:
at least 2 days
Nutritional value:
Analysis per serving, approx:
• 1130kJ/270kcal
• 25g protein
• 17g fat
• 4g carbohydrate

Cut the salmon in half lengthways; remove the backbone and, using tweezers, also remove all the smaller bones. Dry the salmon fillets with kitchen paper. • Combine the salt and sugar. Sprinkle a little of the mixture into a deep square glass or porcelain dish and place one fillet, skin side down, in the dish. Cover the salmon with a good sprinkling of the sugar and salt mixture, then grind some white pepper over the top. Wash and dry the dill, chop finely and scatter over the fillet. Lay the other half of the salmon over the first and sprinkle with more sugar–salt mixture. Cover the salmon with aluminium foil, then place a board on top. Place a weight, a can or similar heavy object, on top. • Leave the salmon in a cool place for at least two days, turning several times during this period. • To serve, place the salmon, skin downwards, on a board, scrape off the dill and seasonings then slice the salmon thinly towards the tail end. Garnish with lemon. • The salmon should be served with a sweet mustard-and-dill mayonnaise made with 4 tbsps hot mustard, 3 tbsps caster sugar, 2 tbsps wine vinegar, 5 tbsps oil and 4 tbsps chopped dill.

Smoked Trout with Horseradish Sauce

350g/11oz celery
1 tbsp lemon juice
2 smoked trout
125ml/4fl oz cream
40g/1 1¹/₂oz freshly grated
horseradish
Pinch each of salt and sugar
1 lemon

Preparation time:
40 minutes
Nutritional value:
Analysis per serving, approx:
• 940kJ/220kcal
• 22g protein
• 13g fat
• 6g carbohydrate

Break the celery into sticks. Trim the root end and the leaves and discard them. Slice the rest into matchstick-sized strips. Arrange the shredded celery on a plate and sprinkle with the lemon juice. • Skin and fillet the trout, removing the smaller bones as you do so. Halve the fillets and arrange into a star shape on the celery bed. • Whip the cream until stiff, add the horseradish and season with the salt and sugar. Take a piping bag with a large star-shaped nozzle and fill it with the cream. Decorate each trout fillet with a small amount of the mixture. • Wash and dry the lemon. Cut thin slices from the centre of the fruit and use as a garnish.

Plaice Rolls in Green Peppers

2 green peppers
Pinch of salt
8 plaice fillets
Juice of 1 lemon
1/2 tsp of salt and white pepper
2 tsps mustard
1 carrot
1 bunch parsley
200g/7oz shrimps in their shells
250ml/8fl oz cream
1 egg yolk
2 tbsps finely chopped fresh dill

Preparation time:
1 hour
Nutritional value:
Analysis per serving, approx:
• 1570kJ/375kcal
• 30g protein
• 23g fat
• 10g carbohydrate

Wash the peppers, halve them and discard the seeds. Do not remove the stalks. Blanch the pepper halves in 250ml/9 fl oz of boiling salted water for 3 minutes, then place them in an oven to keep warm. Retain the blanching liquid. • Wash the plaice fillets and pat them dry. Sprinkle them with lemon juice, salt and pepper and spread them with mustard. Roll up the fillets and fasten them with wooden cocktail sticks. Scrape and chop the the carrot and place it in the blanching liquid with the rolled plaice. Add the parsley and cook over a low heat for 6 minutes. • Place 2 rolls in each pepper half and keep warm. • Wash and peel the shrimps and boil the shrimp shells in the fish and vegetable liquid for 15 minutes. • De-vein the shrimps. • Strain the liquid through a fine sieve and reduce to 125ml/4 fl oz. In a separate pan, reduce the cream by half by boiling over high heat, then stir it into the stock. Beat the egg yolk and use it to bind the sauce; season with a little lemon juice. Add the shrimps and allow them to steep for 2 minutes. • Pour the shrimp sauce over the plaice rolls. Serve garnished with the chopped dill.

Shrimp Omelettes

250g/8oz shrimps
1 tsp lemon juice
1 tbsp finely chopped fresh dill
8 eggs
$^1/_2$ tsp salt
Pinch each of freshly ground
black pepper and freshly grated
nutmeg
25g/1 oz butter
1 dill sprig

Preparation time:
25 minutes
Nutritional value:
Analysis per serving, approx:
• 1130kJ/270kcal
• 24g protein
• 19g fat
• 0.5g carbohydrate

De-vein the shrimps if necessary, and rinse them under cold water. Pat dry with kitchen paper, sprinkle with lemon juice and mix with the chopped dill. • Beat the eggs with 4 tbsps of water and season with salt, pepper and nutmeg. • Heat 20g/$^3/_4$oz butter in a pan, then cook a quarter of the egg mixture for 30 seconds to 1 minute over medium heat. The surface should remain shiny and slightly moist. Slip the omelette on to a heated plate and keep hot. Make three more omelettes from the rest of the butter and the remaining egg mixture. Fill the omelettes with the shrimps and garnish with dill. Serve immediately. • A fresh green salad makes a tasty accompaniment.

Our Tip: *Omelettes should be served as soon as possible after cooking, so try and use several pans simultaneously.*

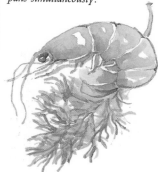

Chinese Deep-fried Scampi

16 peeled giant prawns
½ tsp salt
50g/2oz cornflour
1 egg white
125g/5oz carrots
150g/6oz shelled green peas
2 tbsps oil
250ml/9fl oz tomato ketchup
1 tbsp soya sauce
2 tbsps vinegar
2 tbsps sugar
1 tbsp cornflour
1l/1¾ pints of oil for frying

Preparation time:
40 minutes
Nutritional value:
Analysis per serving, approx:
• 3720kJ/890kcal
• 72g protein
• 50g fat
• 37g carbohydrate

De-vein the prawns. Wash and salt the prawns and toss them in cornflour. Toss the prawns in the lightly beaten egg white and then once more in cornflour. • Heat the oil to 175°C/350°F in the deep-fat fryer. Fry the scampi in portions for about 5 minutes or until golden brown. • Drain on kitchen paper and keep hot. Scrape and wash the carrots, then slice into fine julienne strips. Fry the carrots with the peas in oil. Add the ketchup, soya sauce, vinegar and sugar. Allow to cook for a few minutes. • Mix the cornflour with a little cold water and bind the sauce. • Serve the scampi with the sauce.

18

Flambéed Scampi

16 giant prawns in their shells
1 tsp coarse salt
30g/1oz butter
2 measures Pernod (2¹/₂ tbsps)
1 small clove garlic
250ml/8fl oz cream
Pinch of salt
/₂ tsp freshly ground white
pepper
Pinch each of ground aniseed
and sugar
1 tsp lemon juice
/₂ bunch spring onions
2 tomatoes

Preparation time:
45 minutes
Nutritional value:
Analysis per serving, approx:
2550kJ/610kcal
70g protein
32g fat
11g carbohydrate

Put the prawns in boiling salted water for 3 - 5 minutes. • Remove the shells and intestines. • Heat the butter in a pan and fry the prawns briefly. Pour in the Pernod, set it alight and allow it to burn out. Take the prawns out of the pan and set them aside. Crush the garlic into the frying fat. Thicken with cream and season with salt and pepper, aniseed, sugar and lemon juice. Cook until it acquires a creamy consistency. • Wash the spring onions and cut them into fine rings. Skin the tomatoes by plunging them in boiling water; chop them into quarters, remove the seeds and finally dice the flesh. Put the spring onions and tomatoes in the sauce and bring to the boil briefly. Reheat the scampi in the sauce but prevent further cooking. • Freshly crisped French bread and a fresh green salad with mixed herbs round the dish off perfectly.

19

Stuffed Catfish

1 catfish, weighing 1¹/₂kg/3lb
6oz
Juice of 1 lemon
¹/₂ tsp white pepper
200g/7oz mushrooms
2 shallots
¹/₂ tsp salt
200ml/6fl oz crème fraîche
Pinch of white pepper
200g/7oz white bread
1 bunch of chervil
1 egg
Pinch of grated nutmeg

Preparation time:
40 minutes
Cooking time:
35 minutes
Nutritional value:
Analysis per serving, approx:
• 2740kJ/655kcal
• 35g protein
• 45g fat
• 17g carbohydrate

Scale and clean the fish, wash it thoroughly in cold water and pat dry. Remove the fins and gills. Sprinkle the fish inside and out with lemon juice; rub salt into the body cavity. • Clean the mushrooms and chop them finely, then squeeze them out in a kitchen towel: the mushroom juice is not required. Finely chop the shallots, add them to a pan containing the mushrooms, salt and 2 tbsps crème fraîche and reduce, stirring constantly. Cut the crusts off the bread, cut it into cubes and then process in a food processor with the chervil. • Heat the oven to 200°C/400°F/Gas Mark 6. Smear a baking pan with plenty of butter. Mix the cooled mushrooms with the bread, egg and nutmeg. Stuff the fish and secure the body cavity opening with a wooden cocktail stick or fine string. • Lay the catfish in the pan and bake for about 35 minutes on the lowest shelf of the oven. •During the last 15 minutes in the oven, spread beaten crème fraîche over the fish. • Gherkins or cucumber with dill and fried potatoes go well with this.

20

Baked Redfish

1 redfish, cleaned, weighing
about 1½kg/3lb 6oz
4 tbsps lemon juice
3 slices bread
3 cloves garlic
1 bunch parsley
1 tsp salt
Pinch of freshly ground white
pepper
1 tbsp paprika
6 tbsps olive oil
1 untreated lemon

Preparation time:
20 minutes
Baking time:
40 minutes
Nutritional value:
Analysis per serving, approx:
• 1630kJ/390kcal
• 45g protein
• 19g fat
• 6g carbohydrate

Cut the fins off the fish and
scale it, starting at the tail.
Wash it inside and out, dry it
and sprinkle all over with
lemon juice. • Remove the
crusts from the bread and

crumble into fine crumbs.
Chop the garlic finely. Wash
the parsley, shake it dry, then
chop finely and mix with the
garlic. • Heat the oven to
200°C/400°F/Gas Mark 6.
Rub the fish inside and out
with the salt and pepper.
Spread half of the parsley and
garlic mixture in the body
cavity. Lay the fish on the foil.
Mix together the rest of the
parsley, the bread, the paprika
and the oil and spread the
mixture over the fish. • Bake
the redfish for 40 minutes on
the middle shelf. • Wash and
dry the lemon and cut into
wedges. Serve with a lemon
garnish. • Delicious with fried
potatoes seasoned with thyme
and bay leaf, and a fresh green
salad.

Foil-Baked Cod

800g/1lb12oz cod from the
tail of the fish
Juice of 1 lemon
1 tsp salt
Pinch of freshly ground white
pepper
1 tsp medium hot mustard
100g/4oz spring onions
100g/4oz leeks
100g/4oz carrots
1 bunch of parsley
45g/1¹/₂oz butter
50g/2oz thinly sliced streaky
bacon

Preparation time:
20 minutes
Cooking time:
30 minutes
Nutritional value:
Analysis per serving, approx:
• 1480kJ/350kcal
• 38g protein
• 19g fat
• 7g carbohydrate

Heat the oven to
200°C/400°F/Gas Mark
6. • Thoroughly wash the fish
inside and out with cold water,
dry the fish and sprinkle with
lemon juice. Mix the salt and
pepper and season the inside of
the fish. Spread the mustard
over the skin. • Clean the leeks
and onions and cut them into
rings. Scrape the carrot and
slice into matchstick-sized
strips. Wash the parsley and
shake it dry, then chop it. •
Grease the aluminium foil with
a little butter and lay the fish
on it. Fill the body cavity of
the cod with half the vegetable
mixture and scatter the rest
over the top with the parsley.
Place the bacon on top and dot
with butter. • Loosely seal the
foil around the fish. Place the
package in a flameproof dish
and bake for about 30 minutes
on the middle shelf of the
oven. • Ten minutes before
the fish is cooked open the
foil, remove the bacon and let
the fish brown a little. • Serve
in the foil. • Goes well with
potatoes in parsley and a fresh
mixed salad.

Coley with Tomatoes

To serve 6:
1¹/₂kg/3lb 6oz coley
1 tbsp lemon juice
1 onion
8 tomatoes
1 large potato
Salt and white pepper
2 tbsps oil
50g/2oz fat bacon, thinly
sliced
250ml/9fl oz meat or
vegetable stock
¹/₂ tsp dried basil
250ml/9fl oz sour cream
Some fresh basil leaves

Preparation time:
40 minutes
Cooking time:
about 40 minutes
Nutritional value:
Analysis per serving, approx:
• 1655kJ/395kcal
• 50g protein
• 17g fat
• 10g carbohydrate

Wash the fish inside and out under cold running water; dry on kitchen paper. In each flank of the fish, make two cuts, reaching almost to the backbone, then rub the fish with lemon juice. • Slice the onion into fine rings. Skin the tomatoes by cutting a cross in the skin top and bottom, then immersing them in boiling water for about 2 minutes. Cut the skinned tomatoes into quarters and remove the hard knot where the stalk joins the fruit. • Heat the oven to 200°C/400°F/Gas Mark 6. • Peel and wash the potatoes. • Dry the fish and rub the inside with salt. • Heat the oil in a large pan and fry the onion rings until transparent, turning constantly. • Push the potato into the body cavity of the fish and place it in the pan; the potato will help to balance the fish so that it does not fall over in the pan. • Cover the fish

with slices of bacon. Bake the coley on the bottom shelf of the oven for about 40 minutes. • Heat the meat or vegetable stock. Pour half of it around the fish after 10 minutes in the oven. Surround the fish with the tomatoes. Gradually add the rest of the stock as baking progresses. • Remove the bacon rashers after 25 minutes. Add the dried basil to the sour cream. Pour this over the fish and bake for another 10 to 15 minutes. The fish should end up a crisp, golden brown. •

Dice the bacon rashers. Wash and dry the basil, then cut into thin strips. • Arrange the baked fish on a heated serving dish. Spoon the sauce out of the pan with the onion rings and tomatoes, seasoning with salt and freshly ground white pepper to taste. Top with a scattering of bacon and basil strips. • Delicious with fried potatoes or mashed potatoes and a pea and sweetcorn salad.

Our Tip: *Cod can also be prepared in this way. Instead of the bed of onions, bake the fish over a bed of diced potato. Substitute the sour cream for a sprinkling of breadcrumbs mixed with finely chopped parsley and garlic, and dot with butter. Haddock is good baked on chopped mixed vegetables - carrots, leeks, peas and cauliflower for instance. Use a breadcrumb mixture in the same way as for cod.*

25

Arabian-style Perch

To serve 6:
1 perch weighing about
1½kg/3lb 6oz
3 tsps salt
150ml/8fl oz olive oil
3 onions
1 green pepper
50g/2oz shelled walnuts
3 tbsps finely chopped fresh
parsley
3 tbsps pomegranate seeds or
200g/7oz grapes
½ tsp black pepper
3 cloves garlic
100g/4oz tahini
4 tbsps lemon juice

Preparation time:
30 minutes
Cooking time:
50 minutes
Nutritional value:
Analysis per serving, approx:
• 2415kJ/575kcal
• 51g protein
• 36g fat
• 9g carbohydrate

Wash the fish thoroughly, pat it dry and rub with 1 tsp of the salt. Grease a flameproof dish with half the oil. Toss the fish in the oil and leave to marinate for 15 minutes. • Heat the oven to 200°C/400°F/Gas Mark 6. • For the stuffing, dice the onions finely, remove the stalk and seeds from the pepper, then wash, dry and dice it. Take 2 tbsps of oil from the dish and heat in a pan. Fry the pepper and onion over high heat. • Chop the walnuts coarsely and add to the vegetables; fry for a further 5 minutes. Stir in 2 tbsps chopped parsley and a similar amount of pomegranate seeds, or 100g/4oz seeded grapes; season with 1 tsp salt and the pepper. • Stuff the perch and secure the opening in the body with a wooden cocktail stick. Bake the fish for about 50 minutes. • Crush the garlic and

mix with the tahini, the remaining olive oil, 4 tbsps water, the lemon juice and the remaining salt. • Sprinkle the

26

fish with the remaining
pomegranate seeds and parsley.
• Serve with the sesame sauce
and rice.

Russian Salmon Pie

To serve 6:
For the filling:
100g/4oz buckwheat
250ml/8fl oz water
1 tsp sea salt
100ml/3fl oz sour cream
2 onions
200g/7oz mushrooms
50g/2oz butter
Freshly ground black pepper
1 tbsp lemon juice
2 tbsps finely chopped fresh parsley
200g/7oz smoked salmon
4 hard-boiled eggs
For the pastry:
250g/8oz wholemeal flour
¹/₂ tsp each of caraway seed and coriander
50g/2oz soya flour
Sea salt
20g/³/₄oz fresh yeast or 1 envelope dried yeast
1 tsp honey
250ml/8 fl oz sour cream
60g/2oz butter, diced

Preparation time:
1 hour
Cooking time:
35 minutes
Nutritional value:
Analysis per serving, approx:
• 2175kJ/520kcal
• 246g protein
• 26g fat
• 46g carbohydrate

Boil the buckwheat in water with ¹/₂ tsp of the salt for 5 minutes over a gentle heat. Remove the pan from the heat, cover, and leave the buckwheat to swell for a further 30 minutes. • Stir the sour cream into the buckwheat. • Dice the onions. Wash the mushrooms and slice them thinly. • Melt the butter in a pan and fry the onions until transparent. Add the mushrooms, sprinkle with the rest of the salt and some pepper, add the lemon juice and 1 tbsp of finely-chopped

28

parsley. Cover and sweat the mixture for 10 minutes over a gentle heat, stirring occasionally. • Dice the salmon. Mix the cooked mushrooms, diced salmon and the remaining parsley into the buckwheat. Shell the eggs. • To make the pastry, mix the flour with the seasonings, soya flour and salt. Make a well in the centre of the mixture, crumble in the yeast and pour the honey over the mixture. Wait 2-3 minutes until the yeast dissolves, then add the sour cream and knead to a smooth dough. Cover the dough and leave it in a warm place to rise for 40-50 minutes. • Roll out the dough on a floured surface to a thickness of 3mm/$\frac{1}{8}$ inch. Butter a loaf tin. Cut a piece out of the dough for the lid. Line the base and sides of the tin with the pastry; trim any flaps that hang over the sides. Stir the

buckwheat and mushroom mixture with a fork. Cover the base of the lined tin with about half of the filling. Place the eggs on the mixture then spoon in the remaining filling. Cut three holes about 3cm/1 inch in diameter in the lid. Cover the tin with the reserved piece of dough to make the lid and seal it firmly all the way around the edge. Dot the lid with plenty of butter. • Place the pastry on the middle shelf of a cold oven. • Turn the oven to 200°C/400°F/Gas Mark 6. Bake for 30 minutes, switch off the oven and leave for a further 5 minutes. • The pie is at its best when hot or reheated.

Poached Salmon with Caviar Sauce

4 slices of fresh salmon, each
weighing 250g/8oz each
1 tbsp lemon juice
½ tsp salt
500ml/16fl oz water
1 tsp salt
1 bay leaf
1 tsp black peppercorns
250ml/8fl oz dry white wine
200ml/6fl oz double cream
2 egg yolks
2 tbsps dry white wine
60g/2oz black caviar
2 parsley sprigs

Preparation time:
40 minutes
Nutritional value:
Analysis per serving, approx:
• 3010kJ/715kcal
• 53g protein
• 42g fat
• 6g carbohydrate

Rinse the salmon in cold water, dry it, and rub with lemon juice and salt. • Bring the water to the boil with the salt, bay leaf and peppercorns, cook for 10 minutes, then add the wine. • Place the salmon in the stock and poach for 15 minutes over a gentle heat. • Place the salmon on a heated plate, cover and set aside. • Strain the stock, measure out 125ml/4 fl oz, mix it with the double cream and heat, stirring constantly. • Beat the egg yolks and the wine. Beat the hot cream sauce into the egg yolks in a steady stream with a whisk; stir the caviar into the sauce, pour it over the salmon and decorate with a little parsley.

Pike Dumplings in Herb Sauce

750g/1lb 10oz pike trimmings
2 onions
1 bunch mixed herbs
1 bay leaf
Salt and freshly ground white pepper
2 stale bread rolls
250ml/4fl oz milk
500g/1lb 2oz pike flesh
Pinch of grated nutmeg
3 eggs, separated
200g/7oz king prawns
50g/2oz butter
50g/2oz mushrooms
1 tbsp flour
125ml/4fl oz white wine
250ml/8fl oz cream
1 bunch dill

Preparation time:
1¹/₂ hours
Chilling time:
2 hours
Nutritional value:
Analysis per serving, approx:
• 2635kJ/630kcal
• 39g protein
• 38g fat
• 27g carbohydrate

Boil up the trimmings with 1 onion, the herbs, the bay leaf and salt and pepper in a covered saucepan. Strain and set aside. • Grate the crusts off the rolls. Soften the rolls in milk. Dice the pike flesh, squeeze out the rolls and grind very finely in a food processor. Leave to chill thoroughly for 2 hours. •Season the pike meat mixture with salt, pepper and nutmeg. Fold in the egg whites and leave to chill again. • Boil up the fish stock. • Form the fish mixture into dumplings and place in the boiling stock for 10 minutes. Heat the peeled prawns briefly in the stock. • To make the sauce, sweat the remaining diced onion in the butter, add finely chopped mushrooms, dust with the flour and thicken. Add the white wine and stock, cook for several minutes, then thicken with beaten egg yolks and cream. Finally, stir in the chopped dill.

Herring Pie

To serve 6:
600g/1lb 6oz fresh herring
fillets
350g/11oz floury potatoes
Salt
500ml/16fl oz meat stock
100g/4oz long-grain rice
250g/8oz butter
250g/8oz flour
3 hard-boiled eggs
2 bunches of dill
White pepper
1 egg yolk

Preparation time:
1 hour
Baking time:
40 minutes
Nutritional value:
Analysis per serving, approx:
• 1715kJ/410kcal
• 15g protein
• 27g fat
• 26g carbohydrate

Soak the herring filets for 30
minutes. • Peel the
potatoes, cut them into
quarters and boil for 20 to 30
minutes in salted water. •
Bring the stock to the boil; put
the washed rice in the stock,
cover and leave over a gentle
heat for 20 minutes. • Drain
the potatoes, mash, and add
the butter and flour and mix
until smooth. Place in a
refrigerator for 10 minutes. •
Dry the herring fillets and cut
them into strips. Separate the
hard–boiled eggs into yolks and
whites; mash the yolks and
cut the whites into strips. Wash,
dry and chop the dill. • On a
floured surface, roll the potato
dough into one large and one
small disc. • Heat the oven to
175°C/350°F/Gas Mark 4.
Butter a round tin. • Line the
base and sides with the larger
of the two rounds of dough.
Fill the case with alternate
layers of rice, herring strips, dill
and egg yolk; finally sprinkle
with pepper. Cover the filling
with the smaller piece of
dough. Brush the top of the
pie with the beaten egg yolk,
then, using a fork, make a
number of holes in the top.
Bake the pie on the middle
shelf of the oven for 40
minutes. • Delicious with a
fresh green salad and chopped
dill mixed with melted butter.

Plaice en Croûte

450g / 1lb deep frozen puff
pastry
1 lemon
2 plaice fillets (about 800g / 1¼
lbs)
Bunch of dill
2 shallots
250g / 8oz pike fillet (see tip
below)
2 eggs
Pinch each salt and ground
white pepper
200g / 7oz prawns
1 egg yolk
2 tbsps single cream

Thaw pastry for 1 hour
Preparation time: 45
minutes
Bake for 40 minutes
Nutritional value:
Analysis per serving, approx:
• 1930kJ/460kcal
• 39g protein
• 23g fat
• 22g carbohydrate

Remove the puff pastry from the wrapping, cover and leave to thaw for 1 hour. •Scrub the lemon in lukewarm water, dry and scrape off a little lemon peel. Squeeze out the juice. • Rinse the plaice fillets, dry and sprinkle with 3 tablespoons of lemon juice. Rinse the dill, shake dry and chop finely. • If necessary, remove the bones from the pike fillet. Cut the pike into slices, then mince coarsely. Mix with one egg, 2 tablespoons of chopped dill, the chopped shallots, salt and pepper. Cover the pike filling and place in the refrigerator. • If necessary, remove the black intestinal tract running down the backs of the prawns. Rinse the prawns in a colander and leave to drain. •Brush the edges of the pastry sheets with cold water on a floured work top and then slightly overlap them to roll out two large

sheets. • Rinse the baking tray with cold water and lay one sheet of pastry on top. Pat the plaice fillets dry and place one on the pastry sheet, cover with the remaining chopped dill, the pike filling and the prawns. Sprinkle with the rest of the lemon juice and then lay the second fillet on top. •Separate the second egg. Whisk the white. • Lay the second sheet of pastry on top and trim off any surplus pastry with a sharp knife. Brush the edges with the lightly whisked egg white and press together firmly. Roll out the surplus pastry. Cut out scales, fins and a tiny ring for the eye. Heat the oven to 200°C/400°F/Gas Mark 6. •

Beat the egg yolk with the cream and brush on to the pastry as a fixative for the scales, fins and eye. Attach the pastry shapes carefully. • Cook the fish on the middle shelf of the oven for 40 minutes. Take care that the surface does not brown too quickly. If necessary, cover the fish with aluminium foil. • Serve with a white wine and cream sauce and a green salad. Accompany the dish with the same white wine that was used in the sauce.

Our tip: *Fresh salmon is an extravagant but delicious alternative to pike for the filling.*

Mixed Grill

500g/1lb 2oz sardines
5 tbsps olive oil
2 tbsps lemon juice
2 tbsps cognac
1 tsp each finely chopped fresh
or ½ tsp dried thyme and
rosemary
½ tsp freshly ground black
pepper
1 tsp sea salt
1 aubergine
500g/1lb 2oz courgettes
4 tomatoes
2 tbsps wholewheat flour
½ tsp ground fennel seed
20g/¾ oz butter, diced

Preparation time:
40 minutes
Nutritional value:
Analysis per serving, approx:
• 1465kJ/350kcal
• 29g protein
• 17g fat
• 17g carbohydrate

Wash, clean and scale the sardines. • In a shallow dish prepare a marinade from 4 tbsps olive oil, the lemon juice, cognac, thyme, rosemary, pepper and salt. Steep the fish in the marinade. • Wash the aubergine and courgettes and cut them into slices 1cm/½ inch thick. Wash the tomatoes and cut a cross in the top of each. • Combine the flour with the fennel seeds and toss the fish in the mixture. Soak the aubergine slices in the marinade and then toss them in flour. • Heat the grill and cover the rack with foil. • Lay the sardines and aubergine slices on the foil. Toss the courgettes in the marinade and place them on the rack. Also place the tomatoes on the rack and sprinkle them with the remaining olive oil and some salt and pepper. Sprinkle the fish and vegetables with the remaining marinade and season them with salt and pepper. Dot the vegetables with butter. • Cook the sardines and vegetables under a medium grill for 5 minutes. Remove the tomatoes and set them aside to keep hot, then grill the rest of the vegetables and the fish for a further 5 minutes until tender. • Delicious with a potato or rice salad.

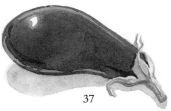

Terrine of Trout

To serve 8:
1 shallot
1 tsp butter
500g/1lb 2oz trout fillets
1/2 tsp salt
Pinch each of freshly ground
white pepper and freshly grated
nutmeg
40g/1¼oz wholemeal bread
250ml/8fl oz cream
100g/4oz very young carrots
15-20 balm leaves
100g/4oz shrimps
2 egg whites

Preparation time:
1½ hours
Cooking time:
50 minutes
Nutritional value:
Analysis per serving, approx:
• 855kJ/205kcal
• 16g protein
• 13g fat
• 5g carbohydrate

Clean and finely chop the
shallots. Heat the butter
and fry the shallots until
transparent, stirring constantly;
then leave to cool. • Wash the
trout fillets in cold water, dry
them and cut into fine strips.
Season with salt, pepper and
nutmeg then mix with the
shallots. Process the mixture in
a food processor. Leave to chill
thoroughly in a refrigerator for
about 20 minutes. • Dice the
bread, pour half of the cream
over it and leave to soak in the
refrigerator. • Scrape, wash and
dry the carrots, then dice them
finely. Wash the balm and dry
on kitchen paper. De-vein the
shrimp. Wash the shrimps,
drain them and chop them
coarsely with the balm leaves. •
Whip the rest of the cream
until stiff. • Beat the egg
whites until smooth and add to
the chilled fish mixture with
the soaked bread. Place the

mixing bowl inside a larger bowl packed with ice cubes. Stir the mixture until it takes on a sheen, then fold in the whipped cream spoon by spoon. • Heat the oven to 125°C/225°F/Gas Mark ¼. Butter the terrine mould or line a loaf tin with buttered aluminium foil. • Mix the carrots and balm into the fish. Transfer the mixture to the mould or tin and smooth the surface. Seal the mould well with a lid or a double layer of aluminium foil. Fill a baking tray half-full with hot, but not boiling, water at a temperature of about 80°C/180°F. Place the terrine in this water bath and cook in the oven for 50 minutes. It is important that the water temperature is maintained at a constant 80°C/180°F. This can be checked with a sugar or roasting thermometer. • Allow the terrine to cool. Cut it into slices of equal thickness just before serving. Portions may be garnished with a wine-flavoured aspic, a few shrimps or balm leaves. To make the aspic, mix and heat equal quantities of clear fish or vegetable stock and dry white wine. Stir in the appropriate amount of softened gelatine. Leave to set in a bowl or in a dish for 3-4 hours.

Halibut and Vegetable Brochettes with Tofu

To serve 6:
1kg/2¼lbs halibut fillets
400g/14oz tofu (soya bean curd)
3 tbsps sesame oil
2 tbsps calvados
4 tbsps dry white wine
1 tbsp soy sauce
1 tbsp apple purée
1½ limes
2 tbsps finely chopped fresh rosemary or 1tbsp dried rosemary
1 each red and green peppers
250g/8oz salad onions
Some lemon balm leaves

Preparation time:
35 minutes
Nutritional value:
Analysis per serving, approx:
• 1295kJ/310kcal
• 40g protein
• 12g fat
• 8g carbohydrate

Cut the fish and tofu into 3cm/1-inch cubes. Prepare a marinade from the sesame oil, calvados, white wine, soy sauce and apple purée. Stir in ½ tsp grated lime rind. Squeeze one lime and add the juice to the marinade with the rosemary. Soak the fish and tofu in the marinade. Cut the peppers into eighths and remove the stalks, seeds and white pith, then wash them and cut them into 3cm/1-inch cubes. Cut the onions in half across, then cut each piece into four. Exchange the fish and tofu in the marinade for the vegetables; leave them to soak for a few minutes. • Heat the grill. • Thread the ingredients alternately onto skewers, and include the balm leaves and a few thin slices of lime. Brush the brochettes occasionally with the marinade as you grill them for 10 minutes.

40

Plaice and Scampi Brochettes

To serve 6:
12 small plaice fillets
12 king prawns
3 tbsps lemon juice
6 small onions
6 tomatoes
18 mushrooms similar in size
1/2 bunch parsley
1 small clove garlic
25g/1oz butter
2 tbsps oil
1/2 tsp dried thyme
1 tsp salt
2 tsps cayenne pepper

Preparation time:
40 minutes
Nutritional value:
Analysis per serving, approx:
• 1755kJ/420kcal
• 70g protein
• 12g fat
• 8g carbohydrate

Wash and dry the plaice fillets. Shell the prawns and de-vein them. Wash the prawns in cold water then drain them. Sprinkle the fillets and the prawns with lemon juice and leave to soak. • Peel the onions and boil them in a little water for 10 minutes. • Cut the tomatoes in half and wash the mushrooms. Wash the parsley and shake it dry. Crush the garlic in a press. • Heat the grill or light the barbecue. • Melt the butter in a pan and mix it with the oil, garlic, rubbed thyme, salt and cayenne pepper. • Cut the onions in half. Place a few leaves of parsley on each of the plaice fillets and roll them up, then thread them onto skewers, alternating with the prawns, tomatoes, onions and mushrooms. • Brush the brochettes with the oil and grill on either side for 5 minutes.

Vichyssoise with Mussels

2 leeks
1 onion
50g/2oz butter
400g/14oz floury potatoes
375ml/14fl oz chicken stock
250ml/8fl oz milk
200ml/6fl oz whipping cream
100g/4oz canned mussels in
brine
200g/7oz shelled prawns
1 tsp salt
Generous pinch of freshly
ground white pepper
Bunch of dill

Preparation time:
40 minutes
Cooking time:
30 minutes
Nutritional value:
Analysis per serving, approx:
• 2000kJ/480kcal
• 22g protein
• 30g fat
• 27g carbohydrate

Remove the root end and the green leaves from the leeks. Halve the white parts and rinse thoroughly. Cut into thin strips. • Peel and chop the onion. • Melt the butter in a large saucepan and fry the leeks and onion until golden. Remove from the heat. • Peel the potatoes and cut into 2cm/1-inch cubes. Add the chicken stock and potatoes to the vegetables. Cover and simmer for 30 minutes. • Purée the soup in a blender or press it through a sieve. Add the milk and return to the boil. • Whip the cream. • Add the prawns and mussels, including the liquid from the can. • Season well with salt and pepper. • Wash the dill, spin dry and chop. • Ladle the soup into serving bowls, stir in the whipped cream and garnish with dill.

Cauliflower and Fish Bake

1 cauliflower
150g/5¹/₂oz millet
500ml/16fl oz water
1 tsp five-spice powder
1 tsp garlic salt
600g/1lb 6oz cod fillet
2 tbsps lemon juice
3 tbsps soy sauce
2 tbsps finely chopped fresh
parsley
2 eggs
200ml/6fl oz cream
50g/2oz butter

Preparation time:
40 minutes
Cooking time:
20 minutes
Nutritional value:
Analysis per serving, approx:
• 2530kJ/605kcal
• 41g protein
• 31g fat
• 39g carbohydrate

Clean the cauliflower in lukewarm water and break it into florets. Cook in water for about 15 minutes with the millet, garlic salt and five-spice powder until tender. • Remove the pan from the heat and leave the millet to swell for a further 5 minutes. Strain the vegetables and millet through a sieve. • Wash and dry the fish and cut it into cubes. Mix the lemon juice, soy sauce and parsley in a bowl. Marinate the fish in this mixture. • Heat the oven to 200°C/400°F/Gas Mark 6. Grease a soufflé dish. •Separate the eggs. Combine the vegetables, marinated fish, egg yolks and cream. Beat the egg whites until they stand in stiff peaks, then carefully fold them into the fish and vegetable mixture. Fill the dish, dot with flakes of butter and bake for 20 minutes.

Redfish and Tomato Bake

800g/1lb 12oz redfish fillets
4 tbsps lemon juice
1kg/1¼lbs tomatoes
½ tsp salt
Freshly ground white pepper
1 onion
1-2 cloves of garlic
4 tbsps oil
1 bunch of thyme or ½ tsp
dried thyme
1 bunch basil

Preparation time:
20 minutes
Cooking time:
30 minutes
Nutritional value:
Analysis per serving, approx:
1590kJ/380kcal
40g protein
20g fat
12g carbohydrate

Wash and dry the fish,
then cut it into 3cm/1-
inch strips; sprinkle it with
lemon juice and leave to soak
for 10 minutes. • Wash and
slice the tomatoes, removing
the hard knot where the stalk
joins the fruit. • Heat the oven
to 200°C/400°F/Gas Mark 6.
Butter a soufflé dish. • Arrange
the strips of fish and tomato
slices in alternate bands across
the dish; sprinkle with salt and
pepper. • Chop the garlic and
onion very finely and fry in
butter until transparent. Wash
the fresh thyme and stir the
leaves into the onion and
garlic. If you are using dried
thyme, just rub it and scatter it
over the pan. Top the
tomatoes and fish with the
onion mixture and cover the
soufflé dish with a lid or
aluminium foil. Bake on the
middle shelf of the oven for 30
minutes. • Serve with a
sprinkling of basil leaves cut
into fine strips. • Delicious
with mashed potatoes or rice.

Mussel Risotto

1 onion
1 clove garlic
30g/2oz butter
250g/8oz short-grain rice
500ml/16fl oz chicken stock
250ml/8fl oz dry white wine
125-250ml/4-8fl oz hot
water
1 bay leaf
2 dried chilli peppers
250g/8oz freshly cooked
shelled mussels (from about
1½kg/3lb 6oz mussels in the
shell) or canned mussels
50g/2oz freshly grated
Parmesan cheese
Salt and freshly ground black
pepper
Some fresh basil leaves

Chop the onion and garlic finely. Heat the butter in a pan and fry the onion and garlic until they turn a golden yellow. Add the rice and fry, stirring constantly, then add the stock, wine and water. Add the bay leaf and chillies. Bring to the boil, then leave the rice over a gentle heat for 30 to 40 minutes. • Drain the mussels and stir into the rice 5 minutes or so before the rice is cooked. Remove the bay leaf and chillies. Stir the cheese into the rice. Season well with salt and pepper. Wash the basil, cut it into strips and scatter it over the risotto. • Excellent with a mixed salad and the same white wine used in the dish itself.

Preparation time:
50 minutes
Nutritional value:
Analysis per serving, approx:
• 1985kJ/475kcal
• 17g protein
• 18g fat
• 55g carbohydrate

Fish Roulade

800g/1lb 12oz Savoy cabbage
1 tsp salt
4 redfish fillets, 200g/7oz
each
Juice of half a lemon
4 tbsps crème fraîche
2 eggs
¹/₂ tsp freshly ground white
pepper
2 tbsps mustard
¹/₂ tsp dried basil
2 tbsps sesame oil
125ml/4fl oz white wine
125ml/4fl oz vegetable stock

Preparation time:
40 minutes
Cooking time:
30 minutes
Nutritional value:
Analysis per serving, approx:
• 1800kJ/430kcal
• 45g protein
• 20g fat
• 10g carbohydrate

Clean the cabbage and blanch in boiling salted water for 8 to 10 minutes. • Wash and dry the fillets and chop them coarsely; purée them in a food processor with the lemon juice, crème fraîche, eggs, pepper and 1 tbsp mustard. Rub the basil and mix it into the fish stuffing and season with salt. • Pull 12 to 16 of the outer leaves off the cabbage. Pare down the heavy central stalks. Lay three or four leaves over one another and top with the fish stuffing. Fold the leaves from the side and finally roll up the roulades; secure with fine string and fry all over in 1 tbsp oil. Mix the remaining mustard with the white wine and pour over the roulades. Cover and braise the roulades for 30 minutes. • Chop the rest of the cabbage finely and cook in the remaining oil, with added vegetable stock, for 15 minutes. Season the cabbage with salt and pepper then arrange it with the roulades.

Clam Chowder

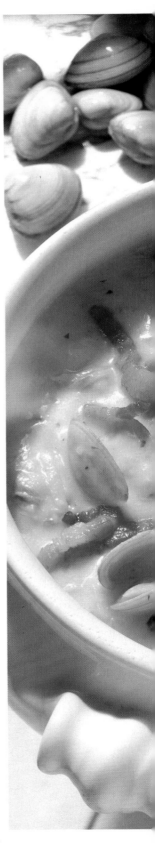

500g/1lb 2oz frozen clams or
200g/7oz canned mussels in
brine
500g/1lb 2oz potatoes
1 large onion
50g/2oz streaky bacon
25g/1oz butter
1 tbsp flour
375ml/15fl oz hot milk
About 250ml/5fl oz hot water
125ml/4fl oz cream
1 tbsp finely chopped fresh
parsley
Salt and freshly ground black
pepper

Preparation time:
1 hour
Nutritional value:
Analysis per serving, approx:
• 1985kJ/475kcal
• 23g protein
• 26g fat
• 37g carbohydrate

Thoroughly wash the frozen
mussels and boil them in a
covered pot with 250ml/8fl oz
of water over a high flame for
3–5 minutes until the shells
open. Shake the pan from time
to time. Remove any mussels
that do not open. • Strain the
mussel stock through a fine
sieve. Drain the canned
mussels as necessary, but
reserve the liquid. • Peel and
dice the potatoes and cook in a
little water for 10 minutes. •
Finely dice the onion and slice
the bacon into strips; fry them
in butter. Stir in the flour and
fry until it turns bright yellow;
gradually add the milk and
mussel liquid. Top up with
water. Allow to boil for 5
minutes. • Strain the potatoes,
purée half of them and then
stir, with the diced potatoes,
back into the soup. Heat
briefly. Add the cream and
parsley and season with salt and
pepper.

Fish Soufflé with Millet

200g/7oz salmon fillet
1 tbsp lemon juice
Pinch of freshly ground white
pepper
$^1\!/_2$ tsp sea salt
100g/4oz carrots
50g/2oz millet
125ml/4fl oz water
6 tbsps milk
2 eggs
1 tsp finely chopped fresh basil
2 tsps arrowroot
Butter for the dish

Preparation Time:
50 minutes
Baking Time:
30 minutes
Nutritional value:
Analysis per serving, approx:
• 690kJ/165kcal
• 15g protein
• 4g fat
• 16g carbohydrate

If necessary, put the fillet of fish in the freezer compartment of your refrigerator for about 10 minutes to make it easier to cut. • Cut the fish into 5mm/$^1\!/_4$-inch cubes and toss in the lemon juice, pepper and salt. • Scrape, wash and dice the carrots and cook in a covered pan over a gentle heat in the water with the millet for 10 minutes. Add the milk. Allow the mixture to simmer for a further 10 minutes, then strain off the liquid. • Heat the oven to 200°C/400°F/Gas Mark 6. Grease an ovenproof soufflé dish. • Separate the eggs. Mix the cooked vegetables and millet with the marinated fish, the basil and the egg yolks. Beat the whites until they form stiff peaks, then fold in the arrowroot. Carefully mix the egg white with the fish mixture. • Fill the soufflé dish and bake for 30 minutes. • Serve immediately.

Redfish Fillet with Bean Sprouts

300g/10oz redfish or cod fillet
4 tbsps lemon or lime juice
2 tbsps soya sauce
2 pinches freshly ground white
pepper
200g/7oz canned bean sprouts
1 tbsp butter
1 tbsp olive oil
2 eggs
100ml/3fl oz cream
1 tsp paprika
3 tbsps chopped chives

Preparation Time:
15 minutes
Nutritional value:
Analysis per serving, approx:
• 1025kJ/245kcal
• 20g protein
• 17g fat
• 2g carbohydrate

W ash the fish, cut into fine strips and mix it with 2 tbsps lemon or lime juice, the soya sauce and the pepper. • Drain the bean sprouts. • Heat the butter and oil in a pan. Fry the bean sprouts for 4 minutes, turning several times. Add the marinated fish and fry it for 3 minutes, stirring regularly. Remove the fish and bean sprouts from the pan and keep them warm. • Beat the eggs with the cream and paprika. Pour this mixture into the pan and stir for 2 minutes while it thickens; stir in 2 tbsps of chopped chives. • Turn the egg out into a heated serving dish. Sprinkle the fish strips and bean sprouts with the remaining lemon juice and spoon them over the egg. Scatter on the remaining chives and serve.

Sweet and Sour Fish

500g/1lb 2oz turbot fillets
Juice of a small lemon
50g/2oz mushrooms
100g/4oz canned bamboo
shoots
2 shallots
4 tbsps sesame oil
2 tbsps flour
Salt
125ml/4fl oz water
1 tbsp each soya sauce and
vinegar
2 tsps sugar
1 tbsp cornflour
1 spring onion

Preparation time:
45 minutes
Nutritional value:
Analysis per serving, approx:
• 670kJ/160kcal
• 22g protein
• 2g fat
• 12g carbohydrate

Rinse the fish fillets in cold water, dry them and cut them into 3cm/1-inch cubes. Sprinkle with lemon juice. • Wash, clean and dry the mushrooms, then slice them thinly. Drain the bamboo shoots and chop finely. Dice the shallots. • Heat the oil in a large pan. Toss the fish cubes in the flour, sprinkle with salt and fry for 6 minutes, stirring all the time. Place the cooked fish on a dish to keep warm. • Fry the prepared vegetables to a golden brown in the remaining oil. Mix together the water, soya sauce, vinegar, sugar and cornflour; stir into the vegetables and allow to bubble up once. Wash the spring onion and cut into fine strips. Tip the vegetables over the fish cubes and scatter onion strips over them. • Freshly toasted and buttered white bread makes an excellent accompaniment.

Our Tip: *Bean sprouts may be used as an alternative to the bamboo shoots.*

Bass in Red Sauce

600g/1lb 6oz bass fillets
2 shallots
3 tbsps cornflour
1 tsp salt
3 tbsps peanut oil
125ml/4fl oz water
$^1/_2$ tsp vegetable stock granules
2 tbsps tomato purée
4 tbsps tomato ketchup
2 tbsps dry sherry

Preparation time:
35 minutes
Nutritional value:
Analysis per serving, approx:
• 920kJ/220kcal
• 27g protein
• 8g fat
• 9g carbohydrate

Wash and dry the fish fillets. Cut lengthwise into slices about 5mm/$^1/_4$ inch thick and crossways into 4cm/2-inch pieces. • Peel and grate the shallots. • Toss the fish slices in a mixture of 2 tbsps cornflour and $^1/_2$ tsp salt.

• Heat the oil in a large pan, stir-fry the fish for 2 or 3 minutes then remove from the pan. • Mix the remaining cornflour with a little water. Bring the water to the boil in a pan. Sprinkle in the stock granules. Stir the grated shallots, the cornflour paste, tomato purée and ketchup into the stock and bring to the boil. • Season this sauce with salt and add the sherry. • Add the fish in the sauce, but do not allow it to cook further. • Serve with firm boiled rice.

53

Cod Cutlets in Tarragon Broth

To serve 8:
8 cod steaks, weighing
250g/8oz each
750ml/1¼ pints water
3 small bay leaves
1 tsp salt
8 peppercorns
2 tsps mustard powder
1 tbsp sugar
3 carrots
6 tbsps tarragon vinegar
300g/10oz shallots
300g/10oz small mushrooms
2 bunches dill
½ tsp white pepper
4 tbsps oil
3 fresh tarragon sprigs

Preparation time:
40 minutes
Marinating time:
1 day
Nutritional value:
Analysis per serving, approx:
• 1190kJ/285kcal
• 46g protein
• 7g fat
• 10g carbohydrate

Wash the cod steaks. Boil the water with the bay leaves and seasonings. Boil the scraped carrots for 10 minutes, then remove them and set them aside to cool. • Put the vinegar and the fish in the stock. Leave the steaks in the bouillon for 8–10 minutes over a low heat, then remove them and set them aside. •Slice the carrots with a crinkle cutter. Wash and slice the shallots and mushrooms. Sprinkle the mushrooms with a little tarragon vinegar. • Strain the fish stock through a sieve and add the prepared vegetables and coarsely chopped dill. Season to taste. • Place the fish in a shallow bowl. Pour the marinade and vegetables over the fish. Sprinkle with oil and garnish with tarragon. • Cover with clingfilm and refrigerate for 1 day.

Marinated Haddock Cutlets

To serve 8:
8 haddock steaks, each
weighing 250g/8oz
4 tbsps flour
125ml/4fl oz oil
2 large onions
2 large carrots
3 cloves garlic
2 bay leaves
1/2 tsp dried thyme
125ml/4fl oz water
750ml/1 1/4 pints herb vinegar
3 tbsps sugar
3 tsps salt
1/2 tsp black peppercorns
20 stuffed olives

Preparation time:
1 hour
Marinating time:
2 days
Nutritional value:
Analysis per serving, approx:
• 1715kJ/410kcal
• 46g protein
• 17g fat
• 16g carbohydrate

Wash and dry the fish steaks, toss them in flour and fry in 4 tbsps of oil for 4 minutes on either side. • Cut the onions into rings and the carrots into strips. Chop the garlic clove finely. • Clean the pan and then fry the onion rings and garlic in the remaining oil until transparent. Stir in the carrot strips, bay leaves and rubbed thyme. Add the water, vinegar, sugar, salt and peppercorns. Boil the stock over a gentle heat for 5 minutes and then pour it over the steaks. • Cover the steaks and refrigerate for 2 days. • Cut the olives in half and scatter them over the fish before serving.

Salt Herrings with Oatmeal

To serve 6:
750g/1lb 10oz salt herrings
(including 1 soft roe)
500ml/16fl oz water
2 bay leaves
10 white peppercorns
2 allspice grains
1/2 bunch pot herbs (turnip,
carrot, leek)
3 shallots
1 tbsp mustard seed
2 tsps dried dill
75g/3oz raw oatmeal
4 tbsps wine vinegar
200ml/6fl oz sour cream
100ml/3fl oz crème fraîche

Baking time:
1 day
Preparation time:
30 minutes
Marinating time:
2 days
Nutritional value:
Analysis per serving, approx:
• 1840kJ/440kcal
• 28g protein
• 31g fat
• 12g carbohydrate

Soak the herrings for 24 hours in plenty of water. Cut the heads and fins off the herrings, then clean and fillet them. • Boil the water containing the bay leaves and seasonings for 15 minutes, strain off the liquid and return it to the pan. • Clean and wash the pot herbs and chop them finely. Peel the shallots and slice them into thin rings, then add them to the stock with the mustard seed, dill and pot herbs. Bring to the boil. • Mix the oatmeal with the vinegar and the sour cream, add it to the stock and boil for 2 or 3 minutes, stirring constantly. Remove the pan fom the stove and stir the crème fraîche and the finely chopped soft roe into the sauce. Allow the sauce to cool a little. Take a large dish with a lid and fill it in layers with the sauce and the herring fillets. • Cover tightly and leave in the refrigerator for 2 days. They will keep for about a week. • Eat with boiled potatoes in their jackets.

Swedish Pickled Herring

*500g/1lb 2oz salted Baltic
herrings
4 shallots
250ml/9fl oz water
1 tsp tea leaves
125ml/4fl oz cider vinegar
2 bay leaves
10 juniper berries
5 black peppercorns
5 allspice grains
5 cloves
2 tbsps olive oil*

Soaking time:
1 day
Preparation time:
30 minutes
Marinating time:
3 days
Nutritional value:
Analysis per serving, approx:
• 1505kJ/360kcal
• 25g protein
• 27g fat
• 4g carbohydrate

Soak the herrings in plenty of cold water for 24 hours.
• The following day, remove the heads and fins, clean them and fillet the fish; finally slice each fillet into pieces about 4cm/1½ inches wide. Slice the shallots into thin rings. • Bring the water to the boil and pour it over the tea leaves; leave to brew for 5 minutes. Strain the tea and leave it to cool, then transfer it to a sealable container. • Add the vinegar, bay leaves, juniper berries, allspice, peppercorns and cloves. Layer the herring fillets so that they are covered by the liquid. Pour the olive oil over the top. • Delicious with potatoes boiled in their jackets or buttered wholemeal bread.

Our Tip: *Leave the Baltic herrings to marinate for 3 days in the refrigerator before use. Then bottle them, in the liquid, in airtight glass jars. They should remain fresh for about 14 days. Making up a larger amount will give you a supply in case of unexpected visitors.*

Bloater Salad with Noodles

To serve 8:
500g/1lb 2oz wholewheat pasta
1 tbsp salt
500g/1lb 2oz green peppers
500g/1lb 2oz tomatoes
400g/14oz gherkins
4 onions, 2 red, 2 white
100g/4oz black olives
500g/1lb 2oz bloaters
2 tbsps olive oil
2 tbsps sunflower oil
4 tbsps red wine vinegar
4 tbsps soya sauce
1 tsp each sea salt and freshly ground black pepper
3 tbsps chive rings
3 tbsps chopped parsley

Preparation time:
25 minutes
Marinating time:
30 minutes
Nutritional value:
Analysis per serving, approx:
• 2090kJ/500kcal
• 26g protein
• 21g fat
• 52g carbohydrate

Boil the pasta for about 10 minutes in 2l/2½ pints of salted water; drain and rinse briefly in cold water. • Cut the peppers into fine strips. Wash and slice the tomatoes. Cut the gherkins into rough cubes and the onions into rings. Chop the olives coarsely. Remove the heads, skin and bones from the fish and break them into pieces. • Put the drained pasta in a bowl with the other ingredients. • Add the oil and vinegar, herbs and seasonings and carefully mix the salad. • Leave the salad for at least 30 minutes before serving.

Mackerel and Bean Salad

To serve 8:

2 tsps vegetable stock granules
1 tsp black pepper
$^1/_2$ tsp ground caraway
$^1/_2$ tsp ground coriander
$^1/_2$ tsp five-spice powder
200g/7oz bulghur wheat
1kg/2$^1/_4$lbs green beans
2 tsps dried savory
4 onions
1kg/2$^1/_4$lbs tomatoes
500g/1lb 2oz smoked
mackerel
2 tbsps olive oil
2 tbsps cider vinegar
1 tsp garlic salt
3 tbsps chopped chives
3 tbsps chopped parsley

Preparation time:
1 hour
Marinating time:
30 minutes
Nutritional value:
Analysis per serving, approx:
• 1340kJ/320kcal
• 20g protein
• 11g fat
• 35g carbohydrate

Bring the stock to the boil with 500ml/16fl oz water and half the herbs and seasonings. Boil the bulghur wheat for 10 minutes in this liquid. Remove the pan from the heat and leave the wheat to swell in the liquid for a further 10 minutes, allow it to cool and then break it up with a fork. • Wash the beans, cut them into 3cm/1$^1/_4$-inch lengths and cook them in a little water with half of the savory for 20 minutes. • Cut the onions into thin rings. Wash the tomatoes and cut them into eighths. Put these vegetables in a bowl with the cooked beans and the wheat and sprinkle with the remaining seasonings. • Remove the heads, skin and bones from the fish, break them into pieces and add them to the vegetables, together with the oil, vinegar, garlic salt and herbs. Leave for 30 minutes before serving.

Shrimp Salad with Rice

To serve 10:
½ tsp salt
100g/4oz long-grain rice
400g/14oz shrimps
100g/4oz almond flakes
200g/7oz canned mandarin oranges
500g/1lb 2oz mayonnaise
125ml/4fl oz single cream
4 tbsps lemon juice
1 tsp medium mustard
3-4 tsps curry powder
¼ tsp freshly grated root ginger
Pinch of sugar
2 apples
125g/5oz gherkins

Preparation time:
45 minutes
Marinating time:
1 hour
Nutritional value:
Analysis per serving, approx:
• 1800kJ/430kcal
• 10g protein
• 34g fat
• 22g carbohydrate

Salt 1l/1¾ pints water and bring it to the boil. Wash the rice and boil it for 12–15 minutes, strain it, rinse in cold water and set aside to drain. • De-vein the shrimps then wash them in cold water and leave them to drain. • Roast the almonds in a dry frying-pan until they turn golden brown, then allow them to cool. Drain the mandarins. • Combine the mayonnaise, cream, lemon juice, mustard, curry powder, ginger and sugar. Wash the apples and cut them into quarters, remove the cores and then slice them thinly; mix the slices into the sauce. Cut the gherkins into fine strips and mix them into the apple mayonnaise together with the rice, mandarin oranges and shrimps. Cover the salad and refrigerate for 1 hour. • Stir in the flaked almonds before serving.

Shrimp and Cucumber Salad

To serve 8:
800g/1lb 12oz shrimps in their shells
1 tsp salt
4 rashers lean smoked bacon
2 tbsps oil
1 cucumber
1 bunch dill
2 tsps medium mustard
½ tsp white pepper
3 tbsps tarragon vinegar
8 tbsps sunflower oil
8 fresh lettuce leaves

Preparation time:
1¼ hours
Nutritional value:
Analysis per serving, approx:
• 1045kJ/250kcal
• 18g protein
• 20g fat
• 2g carbohydrate

Cook the shrimps in boiling salted water for 5 minutes, drain and leave to cool. • Fry the bacon in its own fat until crispy, then dry it on kitchen paper. Break up the bacon into bits once it has cooled. Peel the cucumber, halve it along its length, scrape out the seeds with a teaspoon, then cut each half cucumber into slices 5mm/¼ inch thick; mix it with the bacon. Wash the dill and chop it finely, then sprinkle it over the cucumber. Mix the mustard with a pinch of salt, the pepper and the vinegar. Gradually whisk in the oil as you pour it in a thin stream into the bowl. • Shell the shrimps, de-vein them and add them to the cucumber and bacon mixture. Gradually stir in the marinade. • Allow the salad to marinate for 10 minutes. • Wash the lettuce leaves, shake them dry and use them as a bed for the salad.

Dutch Fish and Potato Salad

To serve 10:
300g/10oz celery
300g/10oz chicory
800g/1lb 12oz boiled potatoes
250g/8oz Dutch cheese in 2 thick slices
800g/1lb 12oz smoked cod
125ml/4fl oz oil
1 tbsp medium mustard
5 tbsps wine vinegar
1 tsp sugar
1 tsp freshly ground white pepper
½ tsp salt
4 onions
2 tbsps small capers
1 bunch parsley
1 bunch chives
4 hard-boiled eggs

Preparation time:
35 minutes
Nutritional value:
Analysis per serving, approx:
• 1730kJ/410kcal
• 31g protein
• 23g fat
• 19g carbohydrate

Remove the root end and leaves from the celery and scrape off the strings. Wash the celery sticks and slice them thinly. Wash the chicory and cut it into slices. Cut the cheese into thin matchstick-sized pieces and the cod into narrow strips. Mix all these ingredients together in a large salad bowl. • Combine the oil, mustard, vinegar, sugar, pepper and salt and pour these into the salad bowl. Dice the onions finely. Chop the capers coarsely. Wash and dry the parsley and chives and chop them finely. Stir these into the salad. • Peel the eggs, cut them into eighths and use them as a garnish for the salad.

Index